THE NATION'S
REPORT
CARD naep

Who Reads Best?

Factors Related to Reading Achievement in Grades 3, 7, and 11

Arthur N. Applebee □ Judith A. Langer □ Ina V.S. Mullis

EDUCATIONAL TESTING SERVICE

ETS®

February 1988

Report No: 17-R-01

CONTENTS

This report, No. 17-R-01, can be ordered from the National Assessment of Educational Progress at Educational Testing Service, Rosedale Road, Princeton, New Jersey 08541-0001.

Library of Congress, Catalog Card Number: 88-60325

ISBN 0-88685-069-X

The work upon which this publication is based was performed pursuant to Grant No. NIE-G-83-0011 of the Office for Educational Research and Improvement. It does not, however, necessarily reflect the views of that agency.

Educational Testing Service is an equal opportunity/affirmative action employer.

Educational Testing Service, ETS, and Ⓔ⒮® are registered trademarks of Educational Testing Service.

ABOUT THIS REPORT

THIS REPORT describes the characteristics and attitudes of certain groups of students in relation to how well they can read. Perhaps more importantly, it details the specific features of reading instruction, how students approach their reading tasks, student reading experiences, and the home and school supports to academic achievement. It does *not* discuss trends over time as many NAEP reports do.*

The variety of possible uses of NAEP data and the multiple audiences interested in these findings define the characteristics, content, and format of these reports.

We hope this report will be useful to teachers looking for evidence to confirm their hunches about good instructional practice. Principals and reading supervisors may find in these pages clues to successes and failures in their own schools and districts. Finally researchers in the field of reading may discover relationships that will suggest new paths to inquiry or support conventional wisdom.

Archie E. Lapointe
Executive Director

*See the Procedural Appendix for further discussion of this issue.

CHAPTER 1
Overview

T HIS REPORT is based on NAEP's 1986 national assessment of the reading achievement of American schoolchildren. The assessment involved nationally representative samples of students in grades 3, 7, and 11 attending public and private schools across the nation. Nearly 36,000 students participated in the reading assessment, which also examined a wide variety of background factors. The present report focuses on those background factors that are most closely related to reading instruction and reading performance, including demographic characteristics, instruction, reading strategies, reading experiences, academic orientation, and home influences.

Nearly 36,000 students participated in the reading assessment . . .

Major Findings

The past two decades have seen considerable change in accepted assumptions about reading instruction in American schools. Recommendations for good teaching include moving from an overwhelming emphasis on basal readers and workbooks toward a greater emphasis on comprehension strategies, a wider range of higher-quality reading materials, more independent reading for children, and more opportunities for combining reading and writing activities.* Such changes in schooling are neither universal nor fully accepted, but they provide a framework for the present discussion of instructional approaches, reading strategies, reading experiences, and student achievement at grades 3, 7, and 11. Several conclusions seem warranted from the results presented in the chapters that follow:

- Students at all three grade levels have particular difficulty with tasks that require them to elaborate upon or defend their evaluations and interpretations of what they have read. Continued attention to such skills must be a major priority in instruction.

- Poor readers report doing less independent reading than good readers. But, in comparison with good readers, they seem to be even more limited in their school reading experiences than in the reading they do on their own. This suggests that poor readers could manage more varied school reading experiences than are currently provided by schools.

- Students at each of the grade levels assessed report that their teachers use a variety of instructional approaches designed to develop appropriate reading skills and strategies, before, during, and after reading.

- However, poor readers report that their teachers use a narrower range of approaches than are used with better readers. The approaches that are used with poor readers are less likely to emphasize comprehension and critical thinking, and more likely to focus on decoding strategies.

- Perhaps as a result, poor readers report using a narrower range of strategies to guide their own reading. The approaches reported by the eleventh-grade poor readers were remarkably similar to those reported by their third-grade peers.

- Results for various demographic subgroups within the population parallel those from earlier assessments. In particular, students from historically at-risk populations continue to perform poorly relative to the national population at each grade level. At grade 11, for example, average proficiency levels for minority and disadvantaged urban students are only slightly above the seventh-grade level for students nationally.

- Reading proficiency is also related to students' general literacy experiences. The more successful readers are likely to be enrolled in academically oriented programs and advanced courses, to spend regular amounts of time on homework each day, and to have home support for reading.

> ... poor readers could manage more varied school reading experiences than are currently provided by schools.

---

*R. Anderson, E. Hiebert, J. Scott, and I. Wilkinson, *Becoming a Nation of Readers: The Report of the Commission on Reading*, The National Academy of Education, The National Institute of Education, and The Center for the Study of Reading, 1985.

The Study

In order to measure students' proficiency, NAEP based the 1986 assessment on a wide range of reading materials and asked questions about students' use of a variety of reading skills and strategies. Thus, the passages and questions in the assessment were diverse. The selections ranged from simple sentences expressing a single concept to complex articles about specialized topics in science or social studies. They included stories and poems as well as essays and reports, selections drawn from beginning reading books and from high school textbooks, and examples of train schedules and telephone bills. Comprehension was assessed in a variety of ways, ranging from multiple-choice questions requiring simple identification of information to open-ended questions asking students to restructure and interpret what they had read and to write out their responses.

For the present report, NAEP used techniques based on item response theory to estimate performance at the three grade levels on a common scale that ranges from 0 to 100, with a mean of 50 and a standard deviation of 10. The scale is useful in making comparisons between grade levels and among subgroups in the population. (See the Procedural Appendix for further information.)

NAEP assessments make it possible to examine relationships between student proficiency and a wide variety of background factors, relating performance to one or two variables at a time. These analyses, however, do not reveal the underlying causes of these relationships, which may be influenced by a number of events. Therefore, the results are most useful when they are considered in the context of other knowledge about the educational system, such as trends in instruction, changes in the school-age population, and societal demands and expectations.

Results for the Nation and Demographic Subgroups

NAEP typically reports results separately for a variety of subgroups defined by such demographic factors as region of the country, gender, race/ethnicity, grade level, and size and type of community. Results for the nation and for these subgroups are displayed in TABLE 1.1.

Average Reading Proficiency for Students in Grades 3, 7, and 11 for the Nation and Subpopulations*

TABLE 1.1

	Average Reading Proficiency		
	Grade 3	Grade 7	Grade 11
Nation	**38.1** (0.2)	**48.9** (0.1)	**56.1** (0.2)
White	**39.8** (0.2)	**50.3** (0.1)	**57.3** (0.2)
Black	**33.4** (0.4)	**45.2** (0.3)	**51.5** (0.3)
Hispanic	**33.2** (0.3)	**44.4** (0.4)	**51.3** (0.3)
Northeast	**39.1** (0.3)	**50.7** (0.3)	**57.4** (0.5)
Southeast	**37.2** (0.3)	**48.1** (0.2)	**54.8** (0.3)
Central	**39.3** (0.4)	**49.0** (0.2)	**56.5** (0.5)
West	**36.9** (0.4)	**48.0** (0.4)	**55.4** (0.4)
Disadvantaged Urban	**31.9** (0.5)	**43.8** (0.4)	**51.2** (0.6)
Advantaged Urban	**41.2** (0.5)	**51.6** (0.4)	**59.5** (0.5)
Male	**37.3** (0.2)	**47.5** (0.2)	**54.5** (0.3)
Female	**38.9** (0.2)	**50.3** (0.1)	**57.7** (0.2)
Upper Quartile	**47.4** (0.1)	**58.2** (0.1)	**67.3** (0.1)
Lower Quartile	**25.9** (0.1)	**38.1** (0.1)	**43.4** (0.1)

*Jackknifed standard errors are presented in parentheses.

Note: For this report, reading proficiency levels and percentages may look similar. Thus, we have adopted the convention of presenting proficiency levels in boldface. These reading proficiency levels are on a *different* scale than the proficiency levels previously reported by NAEP and should not be compared to those results. (See Procedural Appendix.)

Overall, the data indicate an increase in reading proficiency from grade 3 to 7, and again from grade 7 to 11. This pattern of improvement with grade level holds across each of the subgroups sampled.

Parallel to findings in previous assessments, however, at each of the grade levels assessed, White students perform significantly better than their Black and Hispanic peers; students from the Northeast and Central states perform better than those from the Southeast and West; females perform somewhat better than males; and students from advantaged urban communities perform better than those from disadvantaged urban communities. The most distressing aspect of these results is the relatively poor performance of students from at-risk minority groups and from disadvantaged urban communities. At grade 11, average proficiency levels for these groups (Black and Hispanic students as well as students from disadvantaged urban communities) are only slightly above the seventh-grade level for all students nationally.

Table 1.1 also reports average reading proficiency levels for students divided into upper and lower quartiles—those in the top 25 percent in performance and those in the bottom 25 percent.

In these results, perhaps the most interesting feature is that the difference in performance levels between the better and poorer readers remains relatively constant at each grade level. As in previous NAEP assessments, this suggests that American schools continue to have difficulty in narrowing the performance gap between better and poorer readers as they progress through school.*

---

*A. Applebee, J. Langer, and I. Mullis, *Learning to Be Literate in America: Reading, Writing, and Reasoning*, National Assessment of Educational Progress, Educational Testing Service, 1987; *The Reading Report Card, Progress Toward Excellence in Our Schools: Trends in Reading over Four National Assessments, 1971-1984*, National Assessment of Educational Progress, Educational Testing Service, 1985.

CHAPTER 2
Reading
Instruction

RECENT YEARS have seen an increased concern about the critical reading abilities of our nation's students. Although the ability to read thoughtfully has been a continuing goal of reading instruction, a series of studies has indicated that students of all ages are seldom thoughtfully engaged by what they read.* In response to such findings, a strong educational reform movement has arisen, taking as one of its goals that students must learn to reason more effectively about what they read. They must develop the ability to synthesize, analyze, and extend their ideas and their knowledge.

... students must learn to reason more effectively about what they read.

A variety of research efforts extending over the past 15 years have helped us to better understand the nature of the comprehension process and the

---

*A. Applebee, J. Langer, and I. Mullis, *The Reading Report Card, Progress Toward Excellence in our Schools: Trends in Reading over Four National Assessments, 1971-1984*, National Assessment of Educational Progress, Educational Testing Service, 1985; Ernest Boyer, *High School: A Report on Secondary Education in America,* The Carnegie Foundation for the Advancement of Teaching Harper & Row, Publishers, New York, 1983; *A Nation at Risk: The Imperative for Educational Reform*, The National Commission on Excellence in Education, April 1983.

ways it can be taught more effectively.* The concept of reading as an interactive process, with readers bringing meaning *to* the page as much as getting meaning *from* the page, is now accepted in the world of practice as well as research. From this perspective, effective reading instruction entails helping students learn to orchestrate their knowledge of the content and their ways of making sense out of the printed word. In addition to interpreting the information they read based on what they already know, students need to acquire a store of reading strategies from which they can select the most appropriate ones for a particular situation. At the same time, as they read, they need to learn to monitor their developing understanding of a text to ensure that they will leave their reading experiences with the ability to use, describe, defend, or build upon what they have read.

Instructional Approaches:
Before, During, and After Reading

To help students become critical readers, effective instruction focuses on the comprehension process before, during, and after a reading experience. Thus, NAEP's 1986 reading assessment included questions about the frequency with which students were exposed to such instruction. Students were asked to report how often they engaged in a variety of before-, during-, and after-reading instructional activities. For *before*-reading activities, students were asked how often their teachers previewed the material, discussed new and difficult vocabulary, and read new and difficult parts of the text to the students before they read by themselves. For *during*-reading activities, students were asked the frequency with which they were given lists of questions to think about and answer while reading. For *after*-reading activities, students reported on how frequently they were asked to think about, discuss, and support their opinions about the text, to relate ideas to one another, and to identify the main idea of the text after having completed reading.

Students were asked to report how often they engaged in a variety of before-, during-, and after-reading instructional activities.

Grade 3

Third graders' reports on teaching procedures are summarized in TABLE 2.1. Overall, approximately two-thirds of the students in grade 3 reported that their teachers tended to use each of the techniques described above when giving them new things to read. Previewing or giving a general overview of the selection seems to be a particularly widespread activity in third grade classrooms, with only 16 percent of the students reporting that

Landscapes: A State-of-the-Art Assessment of Reading Comprehension Research, 1974-1984. Indiana University, 1985; *Handbook of Reading Research*, P. D. Pearson, editor, New York: Longman, 1984; R. Anderson, E. Hiebert, J. Scott, and I. Wilkinson. *Becoming A Nation of Readers: The Report of the Commission on Reading*, The National Academy of Education, The National Institute of Education, and The Center for the Study of Reading, 1985.

they never engaged in such activities. As many as a quarter of the students claimed that their teachers never pointed out hard words, however, and 31 percent reported that their teacher never read new parts aloud. Nearly 40 percent reported never having received guiding questions to answer while they were reading. While self-report data of this sort are often less reliable for younger than older students, these results suggest that a considerable number of students may not be receiving as much instruction surrounding their reading experiences as might be desirable.

Percentage of Third-Grade Students Reporting Frequency of Teaching Procedures*			TABLE 2.1

	Grade 3		
	Almost Always Percent	About Half of the Time Percent	Never Percent
Before-Reading			
Points out hard words	38.7 (1.2)	35.7 (0.8)	25.6 (1.2)
Previews reading	39.1 (1.1)	45.1 (0.9)	15.8 (1.1)
Reads new parts aloud to class	33.1 (1.0)	35.4 (0.8)	31.5 (1.5)
During-Reading			
Gives lists of questions as you read	29.2 (1.2)	35.0 (1.0)	35.8 (1.4)
After-Reading			
Tells how to find main idea	25.5 (0.8)	51.2 (0.7)	23.2 (1.2)

*Jackknifed standard errors are presented in parentheses.

Grades 7 and 11

Seventh and eleventh graders were also asked to report the frequency with which their teachers used certain instructional techniques when giving students reading assignments. The results are displayed in TABLE 2.2.

TABLE 2.2

Percentage of Seventh-Grade Students Reporting Frequency of Teaching Procedures*

	Grade 7		
	Almost Always Percent	About Half of the Time Percent	Never Percent
Before-Reading			
Points out hard words	32.6 (1.2)	46.0 (0.9)	21.5 (0.9)
Previews reading	44.7 (1.8)	46.3 (1.0)	9.0 (0.8)
Reads new parts aloud to class	41.2 (1.6)	45.7 (0.8)	13.2 (0.8)
During-Reading			
Gives lists of questions as you read	26.1 (1.4)	50.2 (1.0)	23.7 (1.1)
After-Reading			
Tells how to find main idea	14.4 (0.9)	54.4 (0.9)	31.3 (1.3)
Asks how one idea is like another	16.5 (0.8)	62.2 (1.0)	21.4 (1.1)
Asks your opinion	25.7 (1.2)	57.1 (1.0)	17.2 (1.1)
Asks you to support your idea	14.8 (1.0)	61.8 (0.8)	23.4 (1.3)
Has group discuss story	9.0 (0.7)	34.5 (0.7)	56.5 (1.8)

*Jackknifed standard errors are presented in parentheses.

For before-reading activities, there was an increase between grades 7 and 11 in teachers' use of previewing the selection, and a decrease in reading aloud and in attention to highlighting difficult words.

After-reading activities were reported somewhat less frequently. Only 15 percent of the seventh graders and 26 percent of the eleventh graders, for example, reported that they "almost always" were asked to support their ideas. The majority of students did report that they were asked "about half of the time" to relate the ideas they were studying to one another, to express their opinions, and to support their ideas. Nevertheless, because these activities provide students with the greatest opportunity to ponder what they

| | Percentage of Eleventh-Grade Students Reporting Frequency of Teaching Procedures* | | | TABLE 2.2 (continued) |

	Grade 11		
	Almost Always Percent	About Half of the Time Percent	Never Percent
Before-Reading			
Points out hard words	26.2 (1.7)	49.6 (1.1)	24.2 (1.3)
Previews reading	50.6 (1.2)	44.3 (0.8)	5.2 (0.7)
Reads new parts aloud to class	32.2 (1.3)	53.8 (0.9)	14.0 (1.1)
During-Reading			
Gives lists of questions as you read	27.7 (1.5)	56.4 (1.0)	15.9 (1.1)
After-Reading			
Tells how to find main idea	8.5 (0.7)	58.0 (1.1)	33.5 (1.3)
Asks how one idea is like another	26.3 (0.7)	62.8 (0.5)	10.9 (0.5)
Asks your opinion	39.5 (0.9)	51.8 (0.5)	8.7 (0.5)
Asks you to support your idea	26.2 (0.7)	58.0 (0.5)	15.8 (0.5)
Has group discuss story	11.9 (0.4)	43.1 (0.5)	45.1 (0.8)

*Jackknifed standard errors are presented in parentheses.

have read and link it to what they know, it is rather disappointing that students did not report engaging in such thoughtful tasks more frequently. Results for grade 11 are somewhat more encouraging than those for grade 7, with students reporting more emphasis on each of these critical-thinking activities.

The least frequently used after-reading activity reported by the students was the opportunity to discuss what they had read in groups. More than 45 percent of the students at grades 7 and 11 reported never having the opportunity to exchange ideas in group discussion, which can be a powerful context for the development of higher-level thinking skills. Small groups are difficult to manage, however, and some teachers may avoid using discussion groups in large classes.

In general, students' responses to these questions about instructional practices suggest that, while teachers are using a variety of instructional strategies to assist students' comprehension at various stages of the reading experience, even more emphasis on such activities may be desirable.

Supporting Students
with Poorer Reading Performance

In addition to across-age comparisons, it is interesting to examine the instruction received by higher- and lower-performing students within the same age group. TABLE 2.3 displays students' reports about instructional practice separately for students in the upper and lower quartiles of achievement in reading. The patterns that emerge are consistent with previous research indicating that poorer readers receive qualitatively different instruction from their higher-performing classmates.*

... poorer readers receive qualitatively different instruction ...

Students in the upper quartile were more likely to report before-reading activities, although the patterns differed across the grade levels. It appears that in the elementary grades, teachers of betters readers are more likely to preview reading material and read new parts aloud to the class—both activities which emphasize the meaning of the selection. At the middle-school level, better readers reported more exposure to all three types of before-reading activities than did poorer readers. At the high-school level, better readers reported more previewing of material, while poorer readers indicated their teachers more frequently pointed out the hard words and read new parts aloud.

---

*J. Cook-Gumperz, J. Gumperz, and H. D. Simons, *Final Report on Schools- Home Ethnograthy Project*, National Institute of Education, NIE-G-78-0082, 1982; R. L. Allington, "The Reading Instruction Provided Readers of Differing Ability," *Elementary School Journal*, 1983, (pp.255-265).

<table>
<tr><td colspan="2">Percentage of Students in Upper and Lower Quartiles Reporting Frequency of Teaching Procedures Almost All of the Time*</td><td>TABLE 2.3</td></tr>
</table>

	Grade 3 Percent	Grade 7 Percent	Grade 11 Percent
Before-Reading			
Points out hard words:			
Upper Quartile	40.5 (2.4)	38.1 (2.7)	20.6 (2.9)
Lower Quartile	37.9 (1.8)	29.4 (1.6)	31.3 (2.3)
Previews reading:			
Upper Quartile	42.1 (2.9)	52.4 (3.4)	57.2 (2.8)
Lower Quartile	33.2 (3.2)	35.9 (2.1)	43.1 (2.6)
Reads new Parts aloud to class:			
Upper Quartile	41.7 (3.0)	44.6 (2.3)	27.1 (2.6)
Lower Quartile	23.8 (1.9)	33.3 (2.3)	33.6 (2.2)
During-Reading			
Gives lists of questions as you read:			
Upper Quartile	25.8 (1.6)	26.8 (2.8)	28.1 (3.2)
Lower Quartile	34.8 (2.5)	28.7 (2.4)	28.5 (2.4)
After-Reading			
Tells how to find main idea:			
Upper Quartile	19.2 (2.2)	9.2 (1.5)	6.6 (1.5)
Lower Quartile	26.4 (2.6)	23.4 (2.0)	13.8 (1.5)
Asks how one idea is like another:			
Upper Quartile		13.0 (1.5)	31.4 (1.1)
Lower Quartile		21.4 (1.7)	25.0 (0.9)
Asks your opinion:			
Upper Quartile		23.6 (2.1)	47.6 (1.3)
Lower Quartile		27.2 (2.1)	31.5 (0.9)
Asks you to support your ideas:			
Upper Quartile		13.2 (1.4)	31.8 (1.2)
Lower Quartile		17.0 (1.8)	23.5 (1.1)
Has group discuss story:			
Upper Quartile		5.3 (1.1)	11.0 (0.9)
Lower Quartile		15.8 (1.7)	14.2 (0.7)

*Jackknifed standard errors are presented in parentheses.

In contrast, the use of during-reading activities (in the form of lists of questions or study guides) seems similar for upper- and lower-quartile students, particularly at the two higher grade levels. However, at grade 3, there was a tendency for students in the lower quartile to report being given more during-reading activities. It is possible that in the elementary grades, questions to guide silent reading are used most often in remedial reading and with lower reading groups, while the before-reading activities that help prepare students for what they will read are somewhat neglected.

After-reading instructional practices used with better and poorer readers also tend to vary from grade to grade. The only practice asked about at grade 3—finding the main idea—yielded very similar results for better and poorer readers. In the upper grades, however, this became primarily a technique used with poorer readers. In grade 7, poorer readers generally reported more use of the after-reading activities about which they were asked, perhaps reflecting a continuing concern with reading instruction among middle- and junior-high-school students. By grade 11, however, the better readers were more likely than the poorer readers to be asked what their opinions were, to support those opinions, and to indicate how one idea related to another—all activities that may reflect an increasing concern with fostering critical-thinking abilities among these students.

> By grade 11, however, the better readers were more likely than the poorer readers to be asked what their opinions were . . .

In general, younger students and those in the lower quartiles reported being exposed to different instructional procedures less frequently than did older students and those in the upper quartiles. Older students and those in the upper quartiles reported engaging in more before- and after-reading activities than did their lower-performing classmates, and thus may have more opportunities to use the knowledge and experiences they already possess to enrich their reading experiences. They were also more likely to be asked to engage in thought-stretching activities after they have finished their reading of the text. In contrast, their lower-performing classmates seemed to report receiving more assistance in getting through the text. While this help is useful, it may be unnecessarily limiting—keeping students from also beginning to practice the very kinds of reading skills and strategies that are used by their higher-performing classmates.

> In contrast, their lower-performing classmates seemed to report receiving more assistance in getting through the text.

Responding to Reading

In recent years, both researchers and practitioners have been devoting increased attention to the links between reading and writing.* Reading and writing are both activities in which students need to work on building deeper meaning and both call upon similar kinds of knowledge and strategies; good reading and good writing go hand in hand. Further, writing has the potential

---

*Composing and Comprehending, J. Jensen, editor, Urbana, Illinois, National Conference on Research in English/ERIC, 1984; Convergences: Essays on Reading, Writing, and Literacy, B. Peterson, editor, National Council of Teachers of English, Urbana, Illinois, 1986.

to foster deeper and more critical thinking about what a student has read. When students are asked to analyze, interpret, or evaluate what they have read (and to do so in writing), they must not only reason effectively but must also communicate their ideas in ways that others can understand. This sort of critical thinking is often perceived to be at the heart of an academic education. In spite of the importance of such skills, previous NAEP assessments have indicated that while the nation's students have the skills to derive a surface understanding of what they read, they have difficulty when asked to defend or elaborate upon this surface understanding.*

To assess students' ability to read and respond critically, three tasks in the 1986 reading assessment were designed to provide students with the opportunity to read, think, and write; two were stories and one was an expository piece similar to the kind students read for social studies. The three tasks are described briefly below:

"Eggplant" is a humorous piece. After reading it the students were asked to make predictions about character reactions based on what they had read and then to support their responses with details from the original story.

"Goods to Market" is an informative piece. Students were asked to read this social studies passage and to make comparisons between what they had read and their own experiences.

"Jacob," the third item, was given at all three grades. The text follows:

▶ **Questions 9–13.** A student wrote the following story for a school assignment. The story has been typed exactly as the student wrote it. Read the story and then answer the questions based on it.

Paragraph

1   "Jake! Hey Jacob! Come ride your bicycle with me!"

2   I was calling my brother, Jacob, to ask him to bicycle ride with me. I knew he loved bicycle riding almost as much as he loved candy, and cake, and ice cream. Why shouldn't I know! I've known Jacob since he was born five years ago.

3   "O.K. Sarah, I'll bike ride with you, but only if I can bring my Star Wars action figures. They will protect us if a big dog comes," said my brother in a shaky voice. He's afraid of big dogs. He's afraid the dogs will bite him.

continued

*A. Applebee, J. Langer, and I. Mullis, *Learning to Be Literate in America: Reading, Writing, and Reasoning*, National Assessment of Educational Progress, Educational Testing Service, 1987.

continued

4   "You can bring one action figure," I said. "If you bring any more you won't have a hand free to steer your bicycle with."

5   "O.K." Jacob answered once more. That's one of the things I love about my brother. He's so agreeable. In fact, just about the only time he gets mad is when he can't have dessert since he didn't have dinner, or when my sister Rebecca and I tease him if he can't do something like climb a tree as high as us. Then he cries.

6   I hate it when Jacob cries.

7   His mouth puckers up like he's kissing but then his lips quiver, and his nose wrinkles up, and tears stream from his eyes, soaking his brown glasses. His greenish-brown eyes look so sad.

8   When he looks like this I forget why I was teasing him and run up to him and stroke his short brown hair and big ears until he stops crying.

9   "Sarah! Let's go," said my brother. He was getting tired of waiting for me to stop dreaming so that we could start riding.

10   As I got on my big, tan bicycle, and Jacob got onto his small, blue one Jacob asked me, "When we get home can we draw on the sidewalk in chalk? I want to draw superheroes so they can give me rides on their backs."

11   Jacob said this in the high, silly voice he gets when he's happy.

12   "Sure!" I told him.

13   Then we rode off down the street. Just my brother Jacob and I.

9. What do you think is the most important thing the author is trying to say?

_____

_____

_____

10. Explain why you think so.

_____

_____

_____

Students produced their responses under the usual constraints of testing rather than instructional conditions—limited time, no provision for revising their work at some later time, and reading passages that were unfamiliar to them. However, the passages included in the assessment are similar to the type of reading material that students are given in school, making them relatively familiar. As indicated in the following description of the evaluation criteria for the Jacob task, NAEP's scoring reflected the complexity of students' thinking. However, the criteria were lenient, and success at even the highest level did not require extensive understanding or a lengthy response. Still, students had great difficulty expressing even one substantive thought.

For each reading passage, students' responses were evaluated holistically based on their overall success in responding to the questions asked and the defense of their ideas using supporting evidence.

The following student response to the two open-ended questions about the Jacob passage is typical of answers that were rated together as *inadequate*:

9. The author is tring to disgrib Jacob

10. Because the story is telling about Jacob.

Responses that were rated as *minimal* either did not answer the question, or made irrelevant, inappropriate, or overgeneralized comments. A typical example looked like this:

9.

I think he his trying to say is the poys are friends and the way tha~ act

10.

> _because they act so_
> _silly and that stupid voice_
> _he gate whe he is happy_

In contrast, a *satisfactory* response included an interpretation or generalization and one appropriate reason, such as:

9.

> _I think the author is trying to say is she_
> _bues her brother._

10.

> _I think so because of the way_
> _she talks about him and the way she_
> _feels towards him._

Responses that went beyond a single reason, stating an interpretation or generalization and providing at least two appropriate reasons or one elaborated reason, were rated as *elaborated*. A typical example follows:

9.

> Be nice and understanding to your little brother. He's small, and he doesn't know any better.

10.

> Because I have 3 little nephews I also have been there myself when I was little.

As in previous assessments, students at all ages had difficulty responding to questions of this sort; results are summarized in TABLE 2.4. As many as 80 percent of the third graders wrote inadequate or minimal responses to the Jacob item, and only 18 percent could produce a satisfactory response. Although the eleventh graders performed with greater success, 36 percent wrote inadequate or minimal responses, and only 22 percent wrote elaborated responses. This is disappointing, because the criteria for the elaborated level required only that the student provide a brief elaborated explanation or two unelaborated reasons—a seemingly simple task for a reader who had understood the passage.

Percentage of Students at Each Level of Response in Writing Based on Reading Passages			TABLE 2.4

	Grade 3 Percent	Grade 7 Percent	Grade 11 Percent
Jacob			
Inadequate	70.0 (1.2)	36.7 (1.4)	20.8 (1.0)
Minimal	10.7 (1.0)	17.7 (0.9)	15.6 (0.9)
Satisfactory	18.5 (1.0)	38.1 (1.1)	41.3 (1.5)
Elaborated	0.8 (0.3)	7.5 (0.8)	22.3 (1.8)
Goods			
No comparison	69.6 (1.5)	36.2 (1.4)	25.6 (1.4)
Unsatisfactory comparison	29.9 (1.5)	60.4 (1.4)	62.9 (1.6)
Minimal comparison	0.5 (0.2)	3.2 (0.5)	9.0 (1.1)
Satisfactory comparison	0.0 (0.0)	0.2 (0.2)	1.6 (0.4)
Elaborated comparison	0.0 (0.0)	0.0 (0.0)	0.9 (0.3)
Eggplant			
Inadequate		16.6 (1.2)	5.8 (0.7)
Minimal		18.8 (1.1)	16.4 (0.9)
Satisfactory		50.4 (1.8)	58.1 (1.4)
Elaborated		14.3 (0.7)	19.7 (1.2)

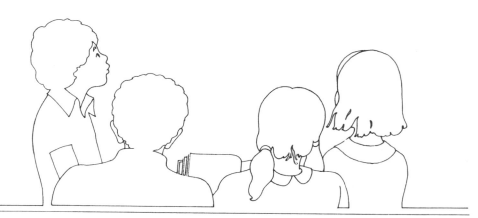

Results for the other two passages were similarly poor, with the social-studies passage proving to be so difficult that 88 percent of the eleventh graders responded at the minimal level or below. Students were apparently unable to relate what they had read to their everyday experiences and make a simple comparison.

These findings are disturbing, but not surprising. They parallel the findings of earlier NAEP reading and writing assessments, which indicated that students in American schools can read with surface understanding, but have difficulty when asked to think more deeply about what they have read, to defend or elaborate upon their ideas, and to communicate them in writing.*

Once again, as in the past few assessments, the conclusion is clear. Reading instruction at all levels must be restructured to ensure that students learn to reason more effectively about what they have read. All students need to develop effective strategies for thinking about, elaborating upon, and communicating what they have learned.

All students need to develop effective strategies for thinking about, elaborating upon, and communicating what they have learned.

---

*A. Applebee, J. Langer, and I. Mullis, *Learning to Be Literate in America: Reading, Writing, and Reasoning*, National Assessment of Educational Progress, Educational Testing Service, 1987; *The Reading Report Card, Progress Toward Excellence in Our Schools: Trends in Reading over Four National Assessments, 1971-1984*, National Assessment of Educational Progress, Educational Testing Service, 1985.

CHAPTER 3
How Students Approach Their Reading Tasks

DURING THE past decade, teachers have become increasingly aware of the importance of providing students with a broad array of strategies for guiding their reading. Teachers have also become increasingly aware that reading involves much more than a process of decoding. It also requires systematic attention to the process of comprehension.

Because of the importance of such strategies, a variety of questions included in the assessment asked students about one or another aspect of their approach to reading. Results from these questions make it possible to examine the extent to which students at different grades are developing an appropriate array of reading comprehension strategies, as well as to examine how better and poorer readers are learning to go about their reading tasks.

To provide an overview of students' general approaches to their reading, one question asked students what they thought about as they read. Responses to this open-ended question were then categorized to reflect the types of student answers. The results are summarized in TABLE 3.1.

What Students Think About When They Read*

	Grade 3		Grade 7	
	Percent	Proficiency	Percent	Proficienc
Comprehension	21.4 (0.7)	**39.8** (0.4)	26.4 (0.9)	**49.8** (0.5
Unfolding of plot	6.7 (0.6)	**42.6** (0.9)	12.8 (0.9)	**50.5** (0.5
Setting and characters	8.0 (0.7)	**41.8** (0.8)	18.3 (0.9)	**51.6** (0.4
Relating story to self	10.5 (0.6)	**41.7** (0.4)	18.3 (1.1)	**51.4** (0.6
Construction of story	2.8 (0.4)	**40.8** (1.0)	4.3 (0.4)	**50.0** (1.1
Reaction to story	6.7 (0.7)	**37.9** (0.8)	6.3 (0.8)	**48.8** (0.7
Decoding	3.0 (0.5)	**39.1** (1.6)	1.1 (0.4)	**46.7** (2.1
No response/Unrateable	43.7		23.4	

Percent of Students

	Grade 3		Grade 7	
	Upper Quartile	Lower Quartile	Upper Quartile	Lower Quartile
Comprehension	25.9 (2.0)	11.4 (1.4)	28.1 (2.3)	20.7 (1.6)
Unfolding of plot	11.2 (2.3)	2.1 (0.6)	16.1 (1.8)	8.2 (1.3)
Setting and characters	11.9 (1.7)	3.4 (0.9)	25.3 (1.8)	9.3 (1.5)
Relating story to self	17.3 (2.0)	4.5 (0.6)	25.6 (2.3)	10.6 (1.3)
Construction of story	3.6 (0.9)	0.8 (0.4)	3.9 (1.2)	3.0 (0.7)
Reaction to story	5.9 (1.1)	6.7 (1.4)	4.2 (0.8)	7.1 (2.5)
Decoding	2.4 (0.7)	1.9 (0.5)	0.9 (0.4)	1.7 (0.7)
No response/Unrateable	24.5	68.6	11.1	43.3

*Jackknifed standard errors are presented in parentheses.

At each of the three grades, comprehension was the most frequent category of response (reflecting 28 percent of the students by grade 11). Other frequent responses involved particular aspects of comprehension, such as an understanding of setting and characters, or attention to the relationships between what students were reading and their own experiences (Relating Story to Self).

Differences in the responses of older and younger readers, as well as be-

TABLE 3.1

	Grade 11	
	ercent	Proficiency
	7.9 (0.9)	56.5 (0.6)
	9.9 (0.7)	55.1 (0.8)
	3.2 (1.3)	58.1 (0.4)
	3.7 (1.2)	58.1 (0.6)
	3.7 (0.9)	57.0 (1.0)
	4.3 (0.6)	53.8 (1.2)
	0.6 (0.2)	57.9 (4.1)
	0.2	

	Grade 11	
	Upper Quartile	Lower Quartile
	1.1 (2.4)	24.1 (2.0)
	8.2 (1.2)	11.7 (2.1)
	1.1 (2.5)	13.4 (1.9)
	0.8 (2.3)	13.9 (1.5)
	0.3 (2.0)	6.5 (1.3)
	2.5 (0.7)	6.8 (1.9)
	0.9 (0.5)	0.5 (0.3)
	9.3	39.2

tween those of better and poorer readers (upper and lower quartiles), are also summarized in TABLE 3.1. The most striking aspect of these comparisons is that older and better readers seemed much more able to articulate what they thought about while they read. Older and better readers were more likely to respond to this question, and when they did respond, drew upon a broader range of responses than did younger and poorer readers. They seemed to have a greater awareness of their own reading processes—a factor which may also help them manage their own reading strategies more effectively.

In addition to asking about general concerns while reading, another question asked about the strategies students might adopt when they found that something was difficult to read. Responses to this question, summarized in TABLE 3.2, indicate a shift in strategies between the lower and upper grades. Among third-grade students, for whom reading is a newer skill, the preferred strategy was to sound out the difficult parts (33 percent), followed closely by asking for help (22 percent). By grade 11, students were more likely to rely on the meaning of the passage as a whole to help them through the hard parts. Twenty-four percent of the students at grade 11 reported that the most helpful strategy was to reread the difficult passage, and another 16 percent reported that they would rely on the context to help them through it.

Most Helpful Approach When Something Is Hard to Read*

	Grade 3		Grade 7	
	Percent	**Proficiency**	**Percent**	**Proficiency**
Sound out	33.0 (1.2)	**37.4** (0.3)	24.6 (1.1)	**48.0** (0.5
Dictionary	10.6 (0.8)	**35.4** (0.6)	12.0 (0.8)	**48.5** (0.6
Ask for help	22.7 (1.4)	**38.9** (0.5)	17.4 (1.0)	**47.0** (0.5
Try to figure it out	14.9 (0.9)	**38.9** (0.5)	13.1 (0.6)	**49.7** (0.7
Reread	4.2 (0.6)	**40.5** (0.8)	13.2 (0.7)	**51.6** (0.6
Use context	6.5 (0.5)	**40.3** (1.0)	11.9 (0.9)	**51.5** (0.5
Never hard	8.2 (0.6)	**37.9** (0.9)	7.8 (0.7)	**50.1** (0.7

Percent of Students

	Grade 3		Grade 7	
	Upper Quartile	**Lower Quartile**	**Upper Quartile**	**Lower Quartile**
Sound out	23.6 (2.0)	45.0 (1.8)	18.0 (1.9)	31.5 (3.0)
Dictionary	5.7 (0.9)	13.5 (1.6)	10.3 (1.4)	15.2 (1.9)
Ask for help	27.0 (2.8)	19.8 (2.1)	10.0 (1.4)	21.2 (2.0)
Try to figure it out	17.0 (1.8)	12.5 (1.3)	14.7 (2.0)	9.9 (1.1)
Reread	7.6 (1.5)	3.3 (0.6)	21.1 (2.0)	7.6 (1.1)
Use context	9.1 (1.1)	6.2 (1.0)	15.6 (2.0)	7.6 (0.9)
Never hard	10.0 (1.7)	11.3 (1.4)	10.3 (1.4)	7.1 (1.3)

*Jackknifed standard errors are presented in parentheses.

... sounding out words was the most popular strategy ...

When the responses of students in the upper and lower quartiles of each grade level are looked at separately, an interesting pattern emerges. At grade 3, although there were some differences in the strategies reported by better and poorer readers, the overall pattern for the two groups was very similar: in both groups, sounding out words was the most popular strategy, followed by asking for help or trying to figure it out. The strategies adopted by the poorer readers show only a little change across the grades (primarily, a slight increase in the proportion who would rely on rereading or context and a slight decrease in the proportion sounding out words or willing to claim that they never found that parts were hard to read). For the good readers, on the other hand, there is considerable development in the approaches they reported, with a shift toward a much greater reliance on the use of context and rereading and away from sounding out or asking for help.

Such a pattern is consistent with recent studies that have suggested 1) that young readers focus on smaller units of text in their quest for meaning, but abandon this as they gain ability to deal with larger text levels* and 2) that better readers are taught more effective reading strategies, while poorer readers are likely to have their old, less-effective strategies reinforced.**

TABLE 3.2

Grade 11

Percent	Proficiency
16.1 (0.9)	**52.3** (0.5)
11.9 (0.8)	**55.3** (0.9)
8.4 (0.8)	**52.9** (0.9)
14.6 (1.0)	**55.1** (0.7)
23.6 (1.3)	**57.8** (0.6)
16.4 (0.8)	**57.5** (0.7)
9.1 (0.7)	**57.3** (1.0)

Grade 11

Upper Quartile	Lower Quartile
8.8 (1.7)	23.9 (2.6)
11.9 (2.1)	14.4 (1.8)
4.3 (1.4)	14.3 (1.9)
12.5 (1.8)	13.5 (2.3)
28.5 (2.8)	13.6 (1.7)
19.3 (2.1)	12.3 (1.7)
14.7 (2.1)	8.0 (1.1)

*J. A. Langer, *Children Reading and Writing*, Ablex, Norwood, New Jersey, 1986

**R. L. Allington, "The Reading Instruction Provided Readers of Differing Ability," *Elementary School Journal*, 1983, (pp. 255-265).

31

Purpose for Reading Stories

The final set of questions related to students' approaches to reading asked about their purposes in reading stories, both in and out of school. Responses to these questions showed some interesting differences between home and school contexts for reading, as well as between better and poorer readers.

When they read for school, students focus on the pragmatic aspects of their reading (TABLE 3.3); they reported that they read primarily to learn something new or to answer questions about what they have read. The balance between these two purposes shifted somewhat across the grades, with learning receiving more emphasis in grade 3 than did answering questions, while at grade 11 answering questions received more emphasis than learning. It appears that as students go through school, both those in the upper and lower quartiles increasingly read to answer particular questions rather than for more general learning or relaxation.

... both those in the upper and lower quartiles increasingly read to answer particular questions rather than for more general learning or relaxation.

Purpose for Reading Stories in School*

	Grade 3	
	Percent	Proficiency
To learn something new	43.9 (1.5)	**39.3** (0.3)
To talk with friends about it	8.3 (0.6)	**33.6** (0.6)
To imagine myself in story	9.2 (0.6)	**34.8** (0.9)
To relax	8.0 (0.6)	**36.3** (0.7)
To answer questions about it	30.6 (1.3)	**39.5** (0.5)

Percent of Students

	Grade 3	
	Upper Quartile	Lower Quartile
To learn something new	48.9 (3.0)	33.9 (1.7)
To talk with friends about it	2.3 (0.6)	13.5 (1.5)
To imagine myself in story	5.0 (1.5)	14.5 (1.7)
To relax	7.3 (1.0)	12.1 (1.7)
To answer questions about it	36.5 (2.3)	26.0 (2.4)

*Jackknifed standard errors are presented in parentheses.

TABLE 3.3

Grade 7		Grade 11	
Percent	**Proficiency**	**Percent**	**Proficiency**
40.6 (1.0)	**48.8** (0.3)	32.1 (1.1)	**57.6** (0.4)
4.5 (0.6)	**44.2** (1.3)	2.0 (0.3)	**50.4** (1.7)
6.6 (0.8)	**46.1** (0.8)	1.7 (0.3)	**48.4** (1.9)
6.1 (0.6)	**46.6** (0.9)	4.5 (0.7)	**55.5** (1.2)
42.2 (1.0)	**49.9** (0.3)	59.6 (1.1)	**57.4** (0.4)

Grade 7		Grade 11	
Upper Quartile	**Lower Quartile**	**Upper Quartile**	**Lower Quartile**
39.7 (2.4)	37.0 (2.5)	34.4 (2.1)	29.1 (2.8)
2.4 (0.9)	9.2 (1.7)	0.3 (0.2)	4.7 (1.2)
4.5 (1.1)	10.4 (1.4)	0.8 (0.3)	4.9 (1.3)
4.3 (0.8)	8.7 (1.4)	3.4 (0.9)	6.6 (1.3)
49.1 (2.2)	34.8 (1.9)	59.2 (2.4)	54.8 (2.8)

Out-of-school reading differed from in-school reading primarily in students' emphasis on reading in order to relax (TABLE 3.4). The proportion of students claiming to read in order to relax or pass the time increased across the grades, from 20 percent at grade 3 to 55 percent at grade 11. The percentage of students reporting that their out-of-school reading was done primarily to learn something new showed a parallel decrease, from 40 percent at grade 3 to 20 percent at grade 11. In this out-of-school reading, the better readers were more likely to emphasize reading to relax, while the poorer readers were more likely to emphasize both reading to learn something new and reading to relax. However, a greater percent of poor readers reported that they did not read outside of school.

> The proportion of students claiming to read in order to relax or pass the time increased across the grades . . .

The results reported in this chapter suggest that most students are learning to treat reading as a process of comprehension and to recognize that it can serve a variety of purposes. For the more proficient readers, this is accompanied by the development of a variety of meaning-making strategies

Purposes for Reading Stories Out of School*

	Grade 3	
	Percent	Proficienc
To learn something new	39.5 (1.3)	**36.7** (0.4
To talk with friends about it	5.3 (0.6)	**33.3** (0.8
To imagine myself in story	12.4 (0.7)	**39.9** (0.8
To relax	19.9 (1.1)	**43.2** (0.4
Don't read out of school	22.8 (0.9)	**36.4** (0.4

Percent of Students

	Grade 3	
	Upper Quartile	Lower Quartile
To learn something new	27.2 (1.8)	45.4 (2.3
To talk with friends about it	2.4 (0.9)	9.6 (1.3
To imagine myself in story	17.4 (2.2)	10.8 (1.6
To relax	39.5 (2.7)	7.8 (1.5
Don't read out of school	13.5 (1.9)	26.4 (1.8

*Jackknifed standard errors are presented in parentheses.

that may help them gain more effective control of the reading process. For the less proficient readers, however, there is less evidence of the development of a broader repertoire of reading strategies. The approaches reported by the eleventh-grade poor readers were remarkably similar to those reported by their third-grade peers.

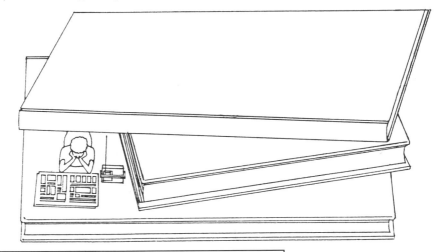

TABLE 3.4

Grade 7		Grade 11	
Percent	Proficiency	Percent	Proficiency
17.1 (0.8)	**46.1** (0.6)	19.8 (1.0)	**55.1** (0.5)
4.4 (0.4)	**45.6** (0.8)	2.3 (0.4)	**50.5** (1.7)
16.2 (0.9)	**48.8** (0.6)	8.2 (0.7)	**57.2** (1.3)
46.8 (1.3)	**51.2** (0.2)	54.5 (1.3)	**59.1** (0.4)
15.5 (1.0)	**45.0** (0.5)	15.1 (1.3)	**53.3** (0.8)

Grade 7		Grade 11	
Upper Quartile	Lower Quartile	Upper Quartile	Lower Quartile
11.7 (1.6)	28.0 (1.7)	13.5 (2.0)	24.2 (2.8)
2.7 (1.0)	7.3 (1.1)	1.1 (0.5)	5.9 (1.5)
13.9 (1.7)	13.1 (1.4)	8.1 (1.7)	9.4 (1.7)
64.8 (2.3)	23.7 (2.2)	67.6 (2.8)	33.8 (2.9)
6.9 (1.2)	27.9 (1.7)	9.6 (1.3)	26.7 (2.8)

CHAPTER 4
Reading
Experiences

They will also develop the interest and motivation to read frequently and widely on their own.

IF OUR schools are successful, students will develop the skills necessary to read a wide range of materials. They will also develop the interest and motivation to read frequently and widely on their own. This chapter will consider the extent to which such goals are being accomplished by examining students' reports about what and how often they read. Because somewhat different questions were asked of third graders than were asked of seventh and eleventh graders, third-grade results will be discussed separately.

Independent Reading at Grade 3

Third graders answered two general questions about the amount of independent reading they do. Results are summarized in TABLE 4.1.

Percentage of Students in Grade 3 Reporting Independent Reading Experiences*

	Daily	Weekly	Monthly	Yearly
How often do you read on your own in school:				
Nation	64.5 (1.2)	20.0 (1.0)	5.3 (0.6)	3.3 (0.3)
Upper Quartile	75.0 (2.4)	18.7 (2.1)	2.3 (0.6)	1.3 (0.5)
Lower Quartile	56.6 (2.5)	19.0 (2.1)	9.2 (1.5)	4.3 (0.9)
How often do you read for fun on your own time:				
Nation	47.9 (1.2)	24.9 (1.1)	7.9 (0.8)	5.5 (0.5)
Upper Quartile	56.2 (2.4)	24.8 (2.1)	6.4 (1.2)	3.7 (0.9)
Lower Quartile	47.6 (2.5)	17.1 (1.6)	9.3 (1.5)	7.0 (1.3)

*Jackknifed standard errors are presented in parentheses.

Overall, a considerable percentage of the students reported daily independent reading, both in school and for fun on their own time. Very few third graders reported doing no independent reading at all, either in school (7 percent) or for fun on their own time (14 percent). There were dramatic differences, however, between the amount of independent reading reported by the better and poorer students, particularly in school. In school, 73 percent of the better third-grade readers reported daily independent reading activities, compared to only 57 percent of the third graders in the lowest quartile. On their own, 57 percent of the better readers reported daily independent reading, compared with 48 percent of the poorer readers.

These results reflect a dilemma. The poorer readers presumably have more difficulty reading on their own and, therefore, are less likely to be encouraged to do so. Yet the fewer opportunities they have to read, the fewer are their chances to become better readers. It is interesting to note that the students' reports indicate more difference between good and poor readers in the amount of independent reading they do in school than in the amount they do on their own. It may be that expectations for the poorer readers are

The poorer readers presumably have more difficulty reading on their own and, therefore, are less likely to be encouraged to do so.

TABLE 4.1

Never
6.9 (0.6)
2.8 (0.9)
10.8 (1.4)
13.8 (0.9)
8.9 (1.0)
18.9 (1.8)

sometimes set too low, asking them to read less than they might be capable of doing.

Variety of Materials

Students need to be encouraged not only to read frequently, but also to read a variety of different kinds of materials. Students' reports on their reading experiences in grade 3 are summarized in TABLE 4.2.

The results in Table 4.2 suggest that third graders' reading is dominated by stories. This is not surprising since reading instruction, which constitutes a significant portion of the school day, relies largely on the use of the basal reader, which is story-based. Substantial proportions of students report that they never read such other materials as newspapers, magazines, biographies, or even comic books. In this case, the reports from the better students suggest that their reading experiences may be even less varied than those of the less-successful readers, who are somewhat more likely to report frequent reading of biographies and comic books.

**Percentage of Students in Grade 3 Reporting
Reading Different Types of Materials***

	Daily/ Weekly	Upper Quartile	Lower Quartile
How often do you:			
Read parts of a story or novel	66.1 (1.3)	73.2 (2.5)	64.3 (2.2)
Read parts of a newspaper	34.3 (0.7)	38.7 (1.7)	32.7 (1.7)
Read parts of magazines	31.5 (0.9)	32.2 (2.2)	32.7 (1.7)
Read biographies	24.1 (0.7)	17.9 (1.5)	28.7 (1.4)
Read sports, travel, hobby books	37.1 (1.1)	35.1 (1.8)	39.2 (2.1)
Read comic books	39.2 (0.8)	31.2 (2.1)	44.4 (1.7)
Look for information in an encyclopedia	39.7 (0.8)	29.3 (1.8)	32.3 (1.3)

*Jackknifed standard errors are presented in parentheses.

Seventh and eleventh graders were similarly asked about the frequency and variety of their reading experiences. Their reports about various types of reading are summarized in TABLE 4.3. Two thirds of these older students reported regular reading of newspapers and magazines, and just under half

**Percentage of Students in Grades 7 and 11
Reporting Reading Different Types of Materials***

	Grade 7				
	At least Weekly	Upper Quartile	Lower Quartile	Never	Upper Quartile
How often do you:					
Read parts of a story or novel	45.0 (0.8)	53.3 (2.1)	36.1 (1.7)	17.9 (0.8)	11.9 (1.0
Read a poem	23.2 (0.8)	21.4 (1.9)	26.3 (1.7)	28.0 (0.8)	22.3 (2.0
Read a play	12.6 (0.8)	8.3 (1.3)	17.6 (1.5)	38.5 (1.3)	31.4 (2.7
Read a biography	12.3 (0.5)	7.2 (1.0)	19.2 (1.5)	41.1 (1.4)	28.7 (2.4
Read parts of a newspaper	67.3 (1.0)	70.0 (1.9)	60.6 (2.2)	12.9 (0.7)	9.3 (1.5
Read parts of a magazine	68.6 (1.1)	72.8 (2.2)	64.5 (2.1)	7.8 (0.5)	2.7 (0.6

*Jackknifed standard errors are presented in parentheses.

TABLE 4.2

Never	Upper Quartile	Lower Quartile
0.1 (1.1)	14.1 (2.4)	23.6 (2.4)
9.6 (1.0)	42.2 (2.7)	53.2 (2.5)
4.0 (1.2)	36.9 (2.5)	46.6 (2.3)
2.7 (1.4)	33.1 (2.9)	46.0 (2.1)
5.8 (1.3)	27.3 (2.6)	39.1 (2.1)
4.8 (1.2)	38.3 (3.0)	33.1 (1.6)
6.4 (1.6)	24.3 (2.4)	42.7 (1.8)

reported regularly reading stories or novels. Other types of reading materials—poems, plays and biographies—remained relatively infrequent choices, even among the eleventh graders.

TABLE 4.3

Lower Quartile	Grade 11					
	At least Weekly	Upper Quartile	Lower Quartile	Never	Upper Quartile	Lower Quartile
23.0 (2.1)	47.6 (1.2)	60.9 (2.7)	32.0 (1.9)	10.6 (0.8)	2.2 (0.6)	21.6 (2.4)
37.6 (1.6)	27.7 (1.2)	28.5 (2.5)	24.9 (1.7)	16.8 (0.8)	7.5 (1.3)	24.5 (1.7)
43.8 (2.2)	8.3 (0.6)	6.5 (1.1)	11.6 (1.3)	34.7 (1.0)	24.1 (2.4)	41.8 (3.1)
63.6 (2.0)	7.5 (0.5)	4.7 (0.9)	10.1 (1.1)	40.3 (1.6)	30.3 (3.0)	49.8 (2.7)
21.5 (1.8)	86.4 (1.5)	88.1 (2.9)	81.0 (2.4)	3.6 (0.6)	3.0 (1.1)	4.9 (0.9)
15.4 (2.0)	78.4 (1.5)	79.9 (2.3)	73.5 (2.3)	2.8 (0.4)	1.2 (0.5)	5.6 (1.3)

To assess the relationship between reading proficiency and independent reading experiences, students' reports about various types of reading were combined into a composite variable reflecting both frequency and variety. The relationship between this variable and average reading proficiency is summarized in FIGURE 4.1 for grades 7 and 11. At both grade levels, the greater the breadth of materials students reported reading, the higher students' reading proficiency was likely to be. The factors shaping such relationships are likely to be complex. On the one hand, students who read more will have more experience in reading and, thus, are more likely to emerge as better readers. On the other hand, better readers may be more likely to read widely both on their own initiative and with the encouragement of their teachers.

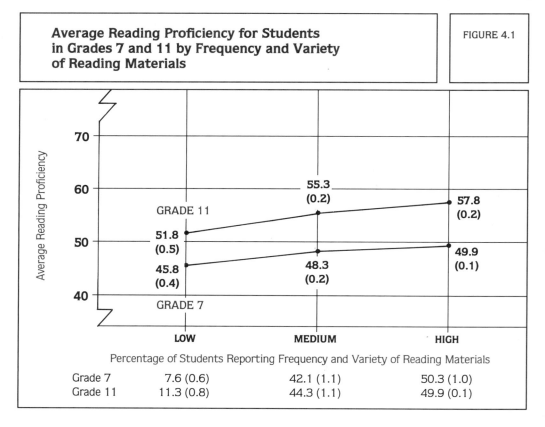

Average Reading Proficiency for Students in Grades 7 and 11 by Frequency and Variety of Reading Materials

FIGURE 4.1

Average Reading Proficiency

GRADE 11

55.3 (0.2)

57.8 (0.2)

51.8 (0.5)

45.8 (0.4)

48.3 (0.2)

49.9 (0.1)

GRADE 7

	LOW	MEDIUM	HIGH
Percentage of Students Reporting Frequency and Variety of Reading Materials

	LOW	MEDIUM	HIGH
Grade 7	7.6 (0.6)	42.1 (1.1)	50.3 (1.0)
Grade 11	11.3 (0.8)	44.3 (1.1)	49.9 (0.1)

Using the Library

The library is a major resource in the development of students' reading abilities. It serves both as a source of reading materials and as a quiet refuge where students can come to read without being interrupted. As part of the assessment of reading habits, students in grades 7 and 11 were asked several questions about their use of the library (see TABLE 4.4).

Percentage of Students in Grades 7 and 11 Reporting Using the Library at Least Monthly*		TABLE 4.4
How often do you go to the library to:	**Grade 7**	**Grade 11**
Read on your own		
Nation	61.5 (1.3)	42.1 (1.4)
Upper Quartile	64.5 (4.0)	47.6 (4.6)
Lower Quartile	58.4 (3.0)	39.8 (3.3)
Look up facts for school		
Nation	60.1 (1.3)	56.1 (1.7)
Upper Quartile	66.2 (3.4)	65.1 (4.1)
Lower Quartile	57.6 (3.5)	47.4 (3.5)
Find books on hobbies		
Nation	42.6 (1.1)	24.0 (1.1)
Upper Quartile	33.3 (3.0)	19.3 (2.2)
Lower Quartile	50.2 (3.3)	29.9 (2.6)
Have a quiet place to read		
Nation	47.6 (1.4)	36.1 (1.3)
Upper Quartile	39.6 (3.7)	38.6 (4.0)
Lower Quartile	56.6 (3.2)	36.4 (3.1)
Take out books		
Nation	73.3 (1.2)	52.0 (1.3)
Upper Quartile	79.5 (3.8)	59.3 (3.7)
Lower Quartile	69.0 (3.5)	42.2 (2.9)

*Jackknifed standard errors are presented in parentheses.

Seventh-grade students reported fairly regular use of the library. Some 73 percent reported taking books out at least monthly, and another 60 to 62 percent reported going to the library to read on their own or to look up facts for school. At the same time, there were interesting differences between how better and poorer readers claimed to use the library. More of the seventh-grade readers in the top quartile reported using the library to read on their own, to look up facts for school, and to take out books. On the other hand, many more of the seventh-grade readers in the bottom quartile reported using the library for a quiet place to read and to find books about their hobbies.

In the eleventh grade, fewer students reported using the library for any purpose, whether to read on their own, to take out books, or to look up facts for school. However, similar to the results at grade 7, there were differences between better and poorer readers in the ways they used the library, with the better readers reporting using the library more frequently for academic purposes and the poorer readers using it more frequently to find out about their hobbies.

> Seventh-grade students reported fairly regular use of the library. Some 73 percent reported taking books out at least monthly.

43

CHAPTER 5
Home and School Support for Academic Achievement

I N ADDITION to specific instructional activities that are designed to foster reading achievement, a variety of other features of school and home environments shape the general context within which students learn to read. This chapter briefly examines the relationships between reading proficiency and two clusters of variables; one reflecting the emphasis on academic achievement within school and the other reflecting home support for literacy. In both cases the results reported here are consistent with those in previous assessments, as well as with results in a long series of previous studies.*

Academic Climate within the School

Many recent calls for educational reform have stressed the need for a more academic emphasis throughout the school years. Such calls have pointed to the need for higher academic expectations and increased coursework for poor-performing and historically at-risk populations, as well as for historically high-achieving groups of students.

In this assessment, eleventh-grade students were asked whether they were enrolled in a general, academic/college preparatory, or vocational/technical school program; they were also asked about their plans after high

---

*D. R. Durkin, *Children Who Read Early*, New York, Teacher's College Press, 1966; T. Raphael and R. Reynolds, editors, *Contexts of Literacy*, New York, Longman, 1986; J. Chall, "Literacy: Trends and Explanations," *Educational Researcher*, 1983, (pp 3-5).

school (see TABLE 5.1). Nationally, some 52 percent claimed to be in an academic or college preparatory program, and a nearly identical percentage planned to go on to a four-year college. Over one half of the White students (54 percent) reported following a academic program, but the percentages of Black and Hispanic students enrolled were smaller (45 and 37 percent, respectively).

Average Reading Proficiency and Percentage of Students in Grade 11 in Various High-School Programs and Their Plans After Graduation*

	Academic	
	Percent	Proficiency
Program of Study		
Nation	51.9 (1.1)	**59.6** (0.2)
White	54.2 (1.0)	**60.6** (0.2)
Black	44.6 (2.0)	**54.4** (0.4)
Hispanic	36.8 (1.6)	**54.7** (0.6)
Upper Quartile	78.0 (1.3)	**66.1** (1.5)
Lower Quartile	27.4 (1.0)	**46.6** (1.4)

	4-Year College		2-Year College	
	Percent	Proficiency	Percent	Proficiency
Plans After High School				
Nation	52.5 (1.1)	**60.1** (0.2)	20.7 (0.6)	**54.8** (0.3)
White	53.1 (1.2)	**61.2** (0.2)	20.9 (0.7)	**55.7** (0.3)
Black	52.1 (1.9)	**54.8** (0.5)	16.4 (1.2)	**50.8** (0.6)
Hispanic	38.2 (1.5)	**55.8** (0.6)	26.9 (1.7)	**51.1** (0.6)
Upper Quartile	78.1 (1.1)	**66.2** (1.5)	12.3 (1.0)	**63.9** (1.8)
Lower Quartile	27.5 (0.9)	**47.1** (1.3)	24.0 (0.8)	**45.9** (1.2)

*Jackknifed standard errors are presented in parentheses.

TABLE 5.1

General		Voc./Tech.	
Percent	Proficiency	Percent	Proficiency
38.1 (0.9)	**52.7** (0.2)	10.0 (0.5)	**50.8** (0.3)
36.8 (0.9)	**53.8** (0.3)	9.0 (0.5)	**52.0** (0.4)
40.5 (1.6)	**49.2** (0.4)	14.9 (1.9)	**48.1** (0.5)
50.6 (2.0)	**49.8** (0.5)	12.6 (2.0)	**48.1** (1.1)
18.9 (1.3)	**63.7** (2.1)	3.1 (0.3)	**62.6** (2.5)
54.8 (1.2)	**44.9** (1.8)	17.8 (1.1)	**44.2** (0.9)

Work		Other	
Percent	Proficiency	Percent	Proficiency
16.9 (0.6)	**51.1** (0.3)	10.0 (0.5)	**52.1** (0.2)
16.8 (0.7)	**52.1** (0.3)	9.2 (0.5)	**53.2** (0.3)
17.9 (1.2)	**47.5** (0.5)	13.6 (1.0)	**48.9** (0.6)
21.1 (1.2)	**47.8** (0.6)	13.8 (1.0)	**48.9** (1.0)
5.6 (0.6)	**62.9** (2.4)	4.0 (0.4)	**63.4** (2.3)
31.6 (0.9)	**44.1** (0.7)	16.8 (1.1)	**44.5** (0.8)

Eleventh graders were also asked about the coursework they had selected in high school. The results, summarized in TABLE 5.2, indicate that the better readers were more likely to have taken more advanced coursework in a variety of subjects, including English, mathematics, and science. Nearly three times more students in the top quartile than in the bottom quartile reported that they had enrolled in advanced coursework. Although these patterns are hardly surprising, they bring to mind such questions as: Would the lower-achieving students have done better if they had been enrolled in more demanding courses in the first place? Does the pattern of course selection and placement reflected in these data simply reinforce patterns of low or under-achievement?

Percentages of Students in Grade 11 Taking Various Courses*		TABLE 5.2

	Upper Quartile	Lower Quartile
	Percent	Percent
Current English Course		
Advanced Placement	27.5 (1.9)	6.7 (0.6)
College Preparation	41.9 (2.3)	15.9 (0.7)
General	29.0 (1.9)	64.0 (1.9)
Remedial	0.3 (0.1)	5.0 (0.6)
None	1.3 (0.4)	4.5 (0.5)
Highest Level of Math Course Taken		
Calculus	13.5 (1.4)	2.2 (0.3)
Algebra 2	63.9 (1.5)	23.6 (1.0)
Geometry	11.9 (0.7)	12.4 (0.8)
Algebra	7.8 (0.7)	22.6 (1.2)
Pre-Algebra	2.8 (0.4)	37.6 (1.3)
Other	0.2 (0.1)	1.6 (0.2)
Highest Level of Science Course Taken		
Physics	11.5 (1.2)	2.6 (0.3)
Chemistry	51.0 (1.5)	14.8 (0.9)
Biology	30.4 (1.1)	55.6 (1.8)
General Science	2.1 (0.2)	19.1 (1.9)
Other	4.9 (0.6)	7.8 (0.6)

*Jackknifed standard errors are presented in parentheses.

The Influence of an Early Start

Another issue in discussions of academic emphasis concerns the age at which school experiences should begin. Two questions in the assessment asked students about their own early school experiences, in particular whether they had attended preschool, nursery, or daycare, and whether they had attended kindergarten. The results are summarized in TABLE 5.3. About one half of the students at all three grade levels reported some type of preschool or daycare experience, and over 90 percent reported that they had attended kindergarten. In general, reading proficiency levels were slightly higher for students who had had such experiences. The NAEP data provide no way to examine the quality of these experiences, however, or the economic factors that may have an effect on why students attend such schools or centers in the first place.

Average Reading Proficiency and Percentage of Students in Grades 3, 7, and 11 Reporting Attendance in Preschool, Nursery, or Daycare*						TABLE 5.3

	Grade 3		Grade 7		Grade 11	
	Percent	Proficiency	Percent	Proficiency	Percent	Proficiency
Nation						
Yes	56.2 (1.1)	**39.4** (0.2)	53.8 (1.0)	**50.0** (0.2)	47.6 (1.1)	**57.3** (0.2)
No	31.9 (1.1)	**36.7** (0.2)	36.6 (0.9)	**48.0** (0.2)	45.8 (1.1)	**55.5** (0.2)
Don't Know	11.9 (0.4)	**35.6** (0.3)	9.6 (0.4)	**46.3** (0.3)	6.6 (0.2)	**52.1** (0.5)

Average Reading Proficiency and Percentage of Students in Grades 3, 7, and 11 Reporting Attendance in Kindergarten*

	Grade 3		Grade 7		Grade 11	
	Percent	Proficiency	Percent	Proficiency	Percent	Proficiency
Nation						
Yes	94.3 (0.4)	**38.3** (0.2)	93.7 (0.5)	**49.1** (0.1)	92.4 (0.5)	**56.3** (0.2)
No	4.3 (0.3)	**34.4** (0.9)	5.0 (0.5)	**45.8** (0.5)	6.5 (0.5)	**53.4** (0.4)

*Jackknifed standard errors are presented in parentheses.

Time Spent on Homework

In addition to questions about early school experiences, course of study, and future plans, students were asked about the amount of time they typically spend on homework each night for all their subjects. Their reports are summarized in TABLE 5.4.

In grades 7 and 11, 10 to 15 percent of the students reported that they were not assigned homework or did not do it, and these students had noticeably lower reading proficiency levels than did their classmates who reported regularly spending time on homework. For those who did homework regularly, however, the amount of time associated with the highest levels of reading proficiency varied somewhat with grade level. At grade 11, students who spent more than two hours per night on homework had the highest average reading proficiency; at grade 7, the highest averages were for students who spent 1 to 2 hours; while at grade 3, there was not a strong relationship between time spent on homework and reading proficiency.

At grade 11, students who spent more than two hours per night on homework had the highest average reading proficiency ...

Average Reading Proficiency and Percentage of Students Reporting Different Amounts of Time Spent on Homework*		TABLE 5.4

	Nation	
	Percent	Proficiency
Grade 3		
Have none	8.6 (0.8)	**38.6** (0.5)
15 minutes	33.7 (0.8)	**37.8** (0.2)
½ hour	26.9 (0.7)	**39.5** (0.2)
1 hour	16.9 (0.6)	**37.7** (0.3)
1 hour +	13.9 (0.6)	**36.1** (0.4)
Grade 7		
Have none	5.1 (0.5)	**46.2** (0.7)
Don't do	5.6 (0.3)	**44.7** (0.4)
½ hour	20.5 (0.6)	**47.6** (0.2)
1 hour	40.2 (0.8)	**49.7** (0.2)
2 hours	19.9 (0.6)	**50.2** (0.3)
2 hours +	8.7 (0.4)	**48.6** (0.4)
Grade 11		
Have none	6.9 (0.5)	**49.8** (0.4)
Don't do	9.3 (0.3)	**52.8** (0.4)
½ hour	18.0 (0.5)	**55.6** (0.2)
1 hour	33.7 (0.4)	**56.4** (0.2)
2 hours	19.9 (0.5)	**57.8** (0.2)
2 hours +	12.2 (0.5)	**58.7** (0.4)

*Jackknifed standard errors are presented in parentheses.

Home Support for Reading

Closely related to high and consistent academic expectations at school is the extent to which students experience a literacy-oriented environment at home. To what extent are books and other reading materials readily available? How much interest is shown in students' school work? TABLE 5.5 summarizes the results on a series of related questions.

| Percentages of Students in Grades 3, 7, and 11 Reporting Home Support for Reading* | | | | | | TABLE 5.5 |

	Grade 3		Grade 7		Grade 11	
Reading Materials in the Home	**Many****	**Few*****	**Many****	**Few*****	**Many****	**Few*****
Nation						
Percent	28.8 (0.8)	40.1 (0.8)	47.1 (1.0)	22.8 (0.7)	62.1 (0.5)	13.4 (0.4)
Proficiency	**40.6** (0.2)	**35.7** (0.2)	**50.6** (0.1)	**45.3** (0.3)	**57.7** (0.2)	**50.8** (0.3)
Upper Quartile						
Percent	39.9 (1.3)	25.8 (1.1)	60.3 (1.3)	11.9 (0.6)	74.6 (1.0)	6.2 (0.5)
Proficiency	**47.8** (0.8)	**45.9** (1.4)	**57.3** (1.1)	**55.3** (1.8)	**65.8** (1.6)	**63.6** (2.3)
Lower Quartile						
Percent	18.8 (1.0)	54.9 (1.4)	33.8 (1.5)	36.7 (1.5)	47.9 (0.8)	24.7 (0.8)
Proficiency	**30.4** (1.4)	**28.7** (1.1)	**41.3** (1.3)	**39.3** (0.9)	**45.9** (1.1)	**43.8** (0.7)
Someone Asks about Schoolwork	**Daily**	**Never**	**Daily**	**Never**	**Daily**	**Never**
Nation						
Percent	67.1 (0.8)	18.8 (0.6)	72.6 (0.8)	9.7 (0.4)	57.6 (0.5)	13.1 (0.4)
Proficiency	**38.5** (0.2)	**36.7** (0.3)	**49.0** (0.2)	**47.5** (0.3)	**56.5** (0.2)	**54.0** (0.4)
Upper Quartile						
Percent	71.3 (1.2)	14.5 (1.1)	74.0 (1.1)	7.9 (0.7)	60.0 (0.8)	9.9 (0.6)
Proficiency	**47.2** (0.9)	**46.2** (1.2)	**56.9** (1.2)	**57.2** (1.1)	**66.5** (1.6)	**65.2** (1.8)
Lower Quartile						
Percent	63.2 (1.5)	21.8 (1.3)	71.5 (1.5)	12.3 (0.9)	53.2 (0.7)	17.1 (0.7)
Proficiency	**29.4** (1.2)	**29.2** (1.2)	**40.6** (1.2)	**39.9** (1.0)	**45.5** (1.0)	**44.2** (0.9)

*Jackknifed standard errors are presented in parentheses.
**Many is defined as including dictionaries, regular newspaper, encyclopedias, regular magazines, and at least 25 books in the home.
***Few is 3 or less of these.

TABLE 5.5
(continued)

Percentages of Students in Grades 3, 7, and 11 Reporting Home Support for Reading*

Family Reads Student Papers	Grade 3		Grade 7		Grade 11	
	Always	Never	Always	Never	Always	Never
Nation						
Percent	55.8 (1.6)	15.2 (0.8)	29.7 (1.4)	18.5 (0.8)	16.0 (0.8)	32.1 (1.4)
Proficiency	**40.0** (0.4)	**36.3** (0.5)	**50.2** (0.4)	**47.4** (0.4)	**57.8** (0.7)	**54.7** (0.6)
Upper Quartile						
Percent	64.7 (2.5)	11.5 (1.4)	35.0 (3.0)	14.1 (1.4)	18.2 (2.0)	26.3 (2.3)
Proficiency	**46.9** (1.0)	**45.9** (1.1)	**57.3** (1.0)	**56.4** (1.1)	**66.8** (1.6)	**66.1** (1.5)
Lower Quartile						
Percent	37.6 (2.0)	20.2 (1.8)	26.1 (2.1)	23.9 (1.8)	11.9 (1.4)	39.9 (3.1)
Proficiency	**30.2** (1.4)	**28.3** (1.2)	**40.8** (1.3)	**39.5** (1.0)	**45.3** (1.6)	**44.3** (0.6)

*Jackknifed standard errors are presented in parentheses.

As has been found in each of the previous NAEP reading assessments as well as in many studies of reading acquisition, the more reading materials available in the home, the better the students' reading proficiency levels are likely to be. Similarly, students whose families pay more attention to school-work and papers are more likely to do well.

In general, the findings from these analyses of school and home support for reading and for general academic achievement indicate that students who have more academically oriented and challenging experiences are more likely to become proficient readers. While this is hardly a new finding, the data remind us that we must continue to strive to provide such supportive environments for all students, including those for whom such experiences are not obviously and easily ready-at-hand.

THE NATION'S
REPORT
CARD

PROCEDURAL APPENDIX

General Background

T HE NATION'S Report Card, the National Assessment of Educational Progress (NAEP), is an ongoing, congressionally mandated project established to conduct national surveys of the educational attainments of young Americans. Its primary goal is to determine and report the status and trends over time in educational achievement. NAEP was created in 1969 to obtain comprehensive and dependable national educational achievement data in a uniform, scientific manner. Today, NAEP remains the only regularly conducted national survey of educational achievement at the elementary-, middle-, and high-school levels.

Since 1969, NAEP has assessed 9-year-olds, 13-year-olds and 17-year-olds attending public and private school. In 1983, NAEP began sampling students by grade as well as by age. The results presented in this report are for students in grades 3, 7, and 11. In addition, NAEP periodically samples young adults. The subject areas assessed have included reading, writing, mathematics, science, and social studies, as well as citizenship, computer understanding, literature, art, music, and career development. Assessments were conducted annually through 1980 and have been conducted biennially since then. Recent assessments have included reading, writing, mathematics, science, computer understanding, literacy, literature, and U.S. history. In the 1987-88 school year, NAEP will assess reading, writing, civics, U.S. history, and geography. All subjects except career development and computer understanding have been reassessed to determine trends in achievement over time. To date, NAEP has assessed approximately 1,300,000 young Americans.

From its inception, NAEP has developed assessments through a consensus process. Educators, scholars, and citizens representative of many diverse constituencies and points of view design objectives for each subject area assessment, proposing general goals they feel students should achieve in the course of their education. After careful reviews, the objectives are given to item writers, who develop assessment questions appropriate to the objectives.

All exercises undergo extensive reviews by subject-matter and measurement specialists, as well as careful scrutiny to eliminate any potential bias or lack of sensitivity to particular groups. They are then field tested, revised, and administered to a stratified, multi-stage probability sample. The young people sampled are selected so that their assessment results may be generalized to the entire national population. Once the data have been collected, scored, and analyzed, NAEP publishes and disseminates the results. Its purpose is to provide information that will aid educators, legislators, and others to improve education in the United States.

To improve the utility of NAEP achievement results and provide an opportunity to examine policy issues, NAEP collects information about numerous background issues; students, teachers, and school officials answer a variety of questions about demographics, educationally related activities and experiences, attitudes, curriculum, and resources.

NAEP is supported by the U.S. Department of Education, Office of Educational Research and Improvement, Center for Education Statistics. In 1983, Educational Testing Service assumed the responsibility for the administration of the project, which had previously been administered by the Education Commission of the States. NAEP is governed by an independent, legislatively defined board, the Assessment Policy Committee.

Content of the 1986 Reading Assessment

The assessment contained a range of reading tasks that measured objectives developed by nationally representative panels of reading specialists and educators.* These objectives combined the work of two Learning Area Committees—those from the 1983-84 and the 1985-86 reading assessments. Many people, including university professors, classroom teachers, legislators, parents, and other interested individuals reviewed drafts of these objectives.

NAEP asked students to read prose passages or poems and answer questions about them. The passages were drawn from a variety of fiction and nonfiction genres. The questions about the passages included a range of traditional multiple-choice items assessing reading comprehension. These questions essentially asked students to locate specific information, to make inferences based on information in two or more parts of a passage, and to recognize the main idea. Many of the questions measured reading for specific information or general understanding. However, since relatively complex interpretative and analytic reading skills are equally important, the assessment also included some open-ended questions asking students to provide written interpretations or short essays based on information that they had read. Responses to these were scored by trained staff using guidelines that focused on the readers' understanding of the information in the passage and their ability to use that information in conjunction with their own knowledge to present an elaboration or extension of what they had read.

*NAEP Reading Objectives, 1986 and 1988 Assessments, The Nation's Report Card, Educational Testing Service, 1987.

Sampling, Data Collection, and Scoring

The 1986 reading assessment was administered to students at age 9/ grade 3, age 13/grade 7, and age 17/grade 11. For this assessment, birth-date ranges for eligible 9-, 13-, and 17-year-olds were defined as October 1 through September 30 for each age level. Thus, the modal grades for those age-eligible students were 3, 7, and 11. NAEP conducted additional sampling of students in these three grade levels to provide nationally representative samples of respondents in grades 3, 7, and 11.

All NAEP assessments are based on a deeply stratified, three-stage sampling design. The first stage entails defining primary sampling units (PSUs) —typically counties, but sometimes aggregates of small counties; classifying the PSUs into strata defined by region and community type; and randomly selecting PSUs. For each age level, the second stage entails enumerating, stratifying, and randomly selecting schools, both public and private, within each PSU selected at the first stage. The third stage involves randomly selecting students within a school for participation in NAEP. Some students sampled (less than 5 percent) are excluded because of limited English proficiency or severe handicap. In 1984, NAEP also began collecting descriptive information about excluded students.

Groups of students were assembled for assessment sessions, with each session lasting about one hour. The 1986 assessment design was based on a powerful variant of matrix sampling called Balanced Incomplete Block (BIB) spiralling. As part of this design, for each subject area (mathematics, science, and computer competence as well as reading) the entire 1986 assessment battery was divided into blocks approximately 15 minutes each, and each student was administered a booklet containing three blocks as well as a six-minute block of background questions common to all students. Six blocks of reading assessment questions were administered at each age/grade level.

As part of the partial BIB design, each pair of blocks within a subject area appeared in at least one assessment booklet. In addition, some blocks were paired across subject areas. At age 9/grade 3, 52 booklets were prepared. Twenty-nine of the booklets contained one or more reading blocks, with each of the six reading blocks appearing in six or seven booklets. Sixty-eight booklets were assessed at age 13/grade 7, with 27 of them containing reading materials and each reading block appearing in six or seven different booklets. Reading items were included in 35 of the 96 booklets administered to students age 17/grade 11, with each reading block appearing seven times.

The spiralling part of the method cycles the booklets for administration so that typically only a few students in any assessment session receive the same booklet. At each age/grade level, each block of exercises is administered to approximately 2,600 students, providing about 2,000 student responses to each item for the grade-level analyses reported herein. Across all the booklets, the results contained in this report were based on 9,793 students at grade 3; 9,513 students at grade 7; and 16,510 students at grade 11.

The 1986 BIB assessment was conducted in February through May using a well-trained, professional data collection staff. NAEP's subcontractor responsible for data collection is Westat, Inc. Quality control is provided through site visits by NAEP and Westat staff members.

After open-ended scoring, the booklets were scanned and the information transcribed to the NAEP data base. These activities were conducted with particular care given to quality control procedures.

Analysis and IRT Scaling

After NAEP data were scored, they were weighted in accordance with the population structure and adjusted for nonresponse. Analyses included computing the percentages of students giving various responses and using item response theory (IRT) technology to estimate proficiency levels for the nation and various subpopulations. IRT methods were used to provide results according to the NAEP reading scale.

The main purpose of IRT analysis is to provide a common scale on which performance can be compared across groups and subgroups whether tested at the same time or a number of years apart. It allows NAEP to estimate performance for any group or subgroup even though all respondents did not take all the exercises in the NAEP pool. All three grade levels were placed on the same proficiency scale, permitting comparisons across grade levels and subpopulations.

IRT defines the probability of answering an item correctly as a mathematical function of proficiency level or skill. NAEP's estimates of statistics describing national and subgroup proficiency are computed as expected values of the figures that would have been obtained had individual proficiencies been observed, given the data that were in fact observed—that is, responses to reading exercises and background items. (For theoretical justification of the procedures employed, see the ETS Research Bulletin "Inferences about latent variables from complex samples." For computational details in the application of NAEP, see *Implementing the New Design: 1983-84 NAEP Technical Report*.)

Why a Different Scale (0-100) for the 1986 Reading Data?

During the analysis process, it was noted that the results of the 1986 reading assessment seemed to be out of line with previous NAEP reading

> All three grade levels were placed on the same proficiency scale . . .

assessment results.* In particular, they indicated precipitous declines in average reading proficiency at ages 17 and 9. The nature of these drops across only a *two*-year period, taken in the context of only modest changes in reading proficiency across a succession of four-year periods since 1971, was simply not believable. It seemed that such a marked drop in reading levels during only two years would have been noticed by teachers and other professionals in education.

The belief that the results were anomalous was reinforced by examining other indicators of achievement that would be expected to show similar declines. No such declines were evident in the mathematics or science assessments administered at the same time. Nor were declines evident in individual state assessments that would have been expected to move in parallel with national results.

We have made every effort to discover any procedural reasons for these results, opening up the problem to scrutiny by NAEP's Technical Advisory Panel, external experts, and the statistical staff at OERI. We have pursued a variety of hypotheses related to potential errors in the sampling, administration, scoring, and scaling, without discovering any problems. Therefore, in consultation with NAEP's Technical Advisory Panel, it was decided that the 1986 reading assessment represents a valid reading test, although no longer anchored to the proficiency levels established in 1983-84. Thus, while it is appropriate to issue this cross-sectional report, it would not be appropriate to use these data to report trends in reading proficiency.

As a result of the inappropriateness of comparing these reading data with previous NAEP reading data, the scale was changed from a 0-500 scale to a 0-100 scale with a mean of 50 and a standard deviation of 10.

We have not, therefore, in this report, described the levels of reading themselves as was done through the NAEP Reading Scale (in a metric of from 0 to 500) in the last reading report. The Reading Scale will be used to track the students assessed in 1984 four years later, in the 1988 assessment. While it is our intention to eventually place the students assessed in 1986 on this Reading Scale, so comparisons in proficiency can be made with past years, the problems we have encountered have caused us to delay issuance of an official trend report until we can conduct the studies necessary to make certain that the assessment we gave in 1986 can be validly compared with previous NAEP assessments. When there is an unprecedented change indicated for such a short period (whether up or down, and in this case down) we believe NAEP should probe deeply into the assessment's data and administration to identify any possible problems in the assessment before we attribute the results to the students; to do otherwise would be irresponsible. The questions which remain about the 1986 reading assessment have to do with the comparability

---

The Reading Report Card: Progress Toward Excellence in Our Schools, Trends in Reading over Four National Assessments, 1971-1984, National Assessment of Educational Progress, Educational Testing Service, 1985.

of this assessment with the prior one, for purposes of measuring trend in proficiency, and not with the accuracy of the results with regard to measuring proficiencies in 1986. Thus, we are confident of the soundness of the results in this report.

For detailed information about the reading data problem, what has been done to investigate the properties of the data, and the studies incorporated into the 1988 assessment, see *The NAEP 1985-86 Reading Anomaly: A Technical Report.*

Estimating Variability in NAEP Measures

The standard error, computed using a jackknife replication procedure, provides an estimate of sampling reliability for NAEP measures. NAEP uses the jackknife methodology to estimate the sampling variability of all reported statistics because conventional formulas for estimating standard errors of sampling statistics are inappropriate for use with NAEP's complex sampling procedures. The standard error is composed of sampling error and other random error associated with the assessment of a specific item or set of items. Random error includes all possible nonsystematic error associated with administering specific exercise items to specific students in specific situations. The estimated population mean ± 2 standard errors represents an approximate 95 percent confidence interval. It can be said with about 95 percent certainty that the performance of the population of interest is within this interval. (For a complete description of the jackknife methodology see *Implementing the New Design: The NAEP 1983-84 Technical Report.*)

NAEP Reporting Groups

NAEP does not report results for individual students. It only reports performance for groups of students. In addition to national results, this report contains information about subgroups defined by region of the country, sex, race/ethnicity, size and type of community, and achievement quartiles. Definitions of these groups follow.

Region

The country has been divided into four regions: Northeast, Southeast, Central and West. States included in each region are shown on the following map.

Gender

Results are reported for males and females.

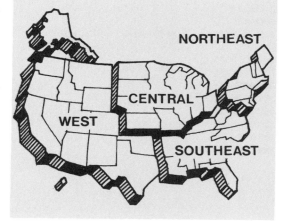

Race/Ethnicity

Results are presented for Black, White, and Hispanic students. Results are based on student self-reports of their racial/ethnic identity according to the following categories: White, Black, Hispanic, Asian or Pacific Islander, American Indian or Alaskan Native, and Other. The sample sizes were insufficient to permit separate reliable estimates for the additional subgroups defined by race/ethnicity. However, all students are included in computing the national estimates of performance levels.

Size/Type of Community

Two extreme community types of special interest are defined by an occupational profile of the area served by a school as well as by the size of the community in which the school is located. This is the only reporting category that excludes a large number of respondents. Although over two-thirds do not fall into the classifications listed below and are not reported in this breakdown, their performance tends to be similar to that of the nation.

Advantaged-urban (high-metro) communities. Students in this group attend schools in or around cities having a population greater than 200,000, where a high proportion of the residents are in professional or managerial positions.

Disadvantaged-urban (low-metro) communities. Students in this group attend schools in or around cities having a population greater than 200,000, where a high proportion of the residents are receiving government assistance or are not regularly employed.

Quartiles

The upper quartile presents average performance for students who were in the top 25 percent on the proficiency level scale; the lower quartile presents average performance for those in the bottom 25 percent.

Additional Background Factors

In addition to the standard NAEP reporting variables of region, gender, race/ethnicity, size and type of community, and the performance quartile variable, NAEP asked all students a number of background questions. Students at grades 3 and 7 were asked about 30 questions and those at grade 11 approximately 50 questions about their school experiences and their home environment including reading materials in the home, level of parents' education, and the time spent on homework.

In addition, background questions specific to reading were included in the reading blocks. Students at all three grade levels were asked questions about their coursework, their reading habits, and the type of instruction they

Students at grades 3 and 7 were asked about 30 questions and those at grade 11 approximately 50 questions about their school experiences and their home environment . . .

59

had received. In addition to containing the results of some of the individual questions asked of all students and of some variables based on combining results to these questions, this report describes results for a composite at grades 7 and 11—"frequency and variety of reading materials."

NAEP initiated the process of developing composite variables by conducting a factor analysis of the results to the background questions specific to reading. This information did suggest a factor at the two higher grade levels associated with reading experiences. Questions were identified and the Weighted Average Response Method (WARM) was then used to create the composite variable. An extension of the Average Response Method (ARM), the WARM technique is appropriate for constructing linear combinations of responses to background questions (i.e., factor scores) when not all sampled students have responded to all questions. (For further information about the ARM and WARM methods, see *Implementing the New Design: The NAEP 1983-84 Technical Report.*)

A Note About Interpretations

Interpreting the results—attempting to put them into a "real world" context, advancing plausible explanations of effects, and suggesting possible courses of action—will always be an art, not a science. No one can control all the possible variables affecting a survey. Also, any particular change in achievement may be explained in many ways or perhaps not at all. The interpretative remarks in this report represent the professional judgments of NAEP staff and consultants and must stand the tests of reason and the reader's knowledge and experience. The conjectures may not always be correct, but they represent a way of stimulating the debate necessary to achieve a full understanding of the results and implement appropriate action.

ACKNOWLEDGMENTS

This report represents the culmination of effort by many experienced and knowledgeable people—staff and consultants who contributed their ideas, time, and energy to the development, conduct, and analysis of NAEP's 1986 reading assessment. Some, because of particularly significant contributions, are specifically thanked below.

The operational aspects of the assessment were managed by Nancy Mead and the complex composition and printing tasks were performed by Peter Stremic. Most of the sampling and data collection responsibility was borne by WESTAT, Inc., whose staff can only be characterized as very dedicated and extremely competent technically. Norma Norris supervised the scoring and created the data base.

Albert Beaton directs NAEP's analysis activities. The reading analyses reported herein were designed and managed by Rebecca Zwick and conducted by Laurie Barnett with assistance from Dave Freund. Consultation on scaling methods was provided by Robert Mislevy and Kathy Sheehan.

Special thanks for the production of this report are due to the many reviewers who suggested improvements. Kent Ashworth and Jan Askew coordinated the production efforts, Beverly Cisney provided word-processing services, Joyce Torrens and Janice Scillia managed composition and proofreading tasks, and Jack Weaver designed and illustrated the report.

Finally and most importantly, NAEP is grateful for the contributions of the students and school administrators who cooperated so generously.

 918-**?**